The GREATEST COUNTRY HITS of 2000

Project Manager: Carol Cuellar
Cover Design: Olivia D. Novak

CONTENTS

ALMOST DOESN'T COUNT *Mark Wills* 4

AMAZED *Lonestar* 14

ANOTHER NINE MINUTES *Yankee Grey* 18

BACK AT ONE *Mark Wills* 9

BECAUSE YOU LOVE ME *Jo Dee Messina* 22

BEEN THERE *Clint Black with Steve Wariner* 30

BEER THIRTY *Brooks & Dunn* 36

THE BEST DAY *George Strait* 40

BREATHE *Faith Hill* 25

BUSY MAN *Billy Ray Cyrus* 44

CAN'T NOBODY LOVE YOU (Like I Do) *Wynonna* 48

THE CHAIN OF LOVE *Clay Walker* 52

CHANGE *Sons of the Desert* 56

COULDN'T LAST A MOMENT *Collin Raye* 60

FAITH IN YOU *Steve Wariner* 64

FALLIN' (Never Felt So Good) *Mark Chesnutt* 68

THE FUN OF YOUR LOVE *Jennifer Day* 72

GONE CRAZY *Alan Jackson* 76

HANDS OF A WORKING MAN *Ty Herndon* 80

HOW FOREVER FEELS *Kenny Chesney* 84

I CAN'T GET OVER YOU *Brooks & Dunn* 88

I HOPE YOU DANCE *Lee Ann Womack with Sons of the Desert* 93

I'LL BE *Reba McEntire* 98

I'LL THINK OF A REASON LATER *Lee Ann Womack* 104

IT MUST BE LOVE *Alan Jackson* 101

IT WAS *Chely Wright* 112

IT'S A BEAUTIFUL THING *Paul Brandt* 115

IT'S ALWAYS SOMETHIN' *Joe Diffie* 120

I'VE FORGOTTEN HOW YOU FEEL *Sonya Isaacs* 108

KEEPIN' UP *Alabama* 125

LET'S MAKE SURE WE KISS GOODBYE *Vince Gill* 130

MORE *Trace Adkins* 138

NO MERCY *Ty Herndon* 133

(Now You See Me) NOW YOU DON'T *Lee Ann Womack* 142

THE QUITTIN' KIND *Joe Diffie* 146

SHE'S MORE *Andy Griggs* 150

SMOKE RINGS IN THE DARK *Gary Allan* 153

SOMEBODY'S OUT THERE WATCHING *The Kinleys* 156

THIS WOMAN NEEDS *Shedaisy* 163

THREE LITTLE TEARDROPS *Joanie Keller* 166

UNBREAKABLE HEART *Jessica Andrews* 174

UNCONDITIONAL *Clay Davidson* 178

WHAT ABOUT NOW *Lonestar* 169

WHEN YOU SAY NOTHING AT ALL *Keith Whitley* 182

ALMOST DOESN'T COUNT

Words and Music by
GUY ROCHE and SHELLY PEIKEN

1. Al - most made you love___

Verse 1:

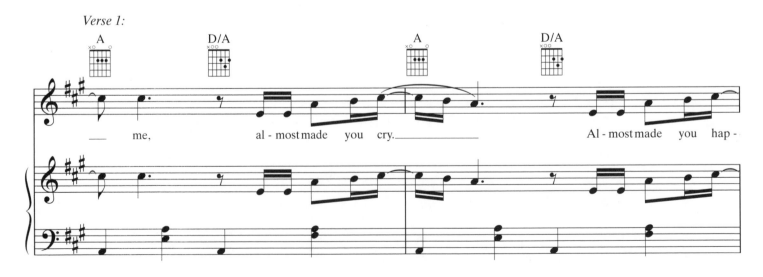

___ me, al - most made you cry._____ Al - most made you hap -

5

Verse 3:
Gonna find me somebody not afraid to let go.
Want a no-doubt, be-there kind of girl.
You came real close.
But every time you built me up, you only let me down.
But everybody knows almost doesn't count.
(To Chorus:)

Verse 4:
Maybe you'll be sorry, maybe you'll be cold.
Maybe you'll come running back
From the cruel, cruel world.
You almost convince me you're gonna stick around.
But everybody knows almost doesn't count.

BACK AT ONE

Words and Music by
BRIAN McKNIGHT

12

AMAZED

Tune guitar down a half step

**Words and Music by
MARV GREEN, AIMEE MAYO
and CHRIS LINDSEY**

Amazed - 4 - 1

Verse 2:
The smell of your skin,
The taste of your kiss,
The way you whisper in the dark.
Your hair all around me,
Baby, you surround me;
You touch every place in my heart.
Oh, it feels like the first time every time.
I wanna spend the whole night in your eyes.
(To Chorus:)

ANOTHER NINE MINUTES

Words and Music by
TIM BUPPERT, BILLY CRAIN
and TOM DOUGLAS

Repeat ad lib. and fade

Verse 2:
I love the way the sunlight
Dances on your perfect skin.
Girl, I wish this night would never end.
But we gotta get moving.
Can't eat if we don't get paid.
But I got us a better idea.
Let's pull up the covers
And stay right here.
(To Chorus:)

BECAUSE YOU LOVE ME

Words and Music by
KOSTAS and JOHN SCOTT SHERRILL

Verse 3:
Instrumental solo ad lib.
(To Bridge:)

Verse 4:
I believe in things unseen;
I believe in the message of a dream.
And I believe in what you are
Because you love me.

Verse 5:
With all my heart
And all my soul,
I'm loving you and I never will let go.
And every day I let it show
Because you love me.
(To Coda)

BREATHE

Words and Music by
STEPHANIE BENTLEY
and HOLLY LAMAR

BEEN THERE

Words and Music by
CLINT BLACK and STEVE WARINER

Been There - 6 - 1

Verse 2:
Did you ever wake up in the middle of the day
And wonder who you are?
You suddenly discover there's a price you pay
For gettin' this far.
And it's the part of you, oh,
You really don't have to spend.
You know I've been there,
And I don't wanna go back again.
(To Bridge:)

BEER THIRTY

Words and Music by
TERRY MCBRIDE and RONNIE DUNN

Moderately fast shuffle ♩ = 124

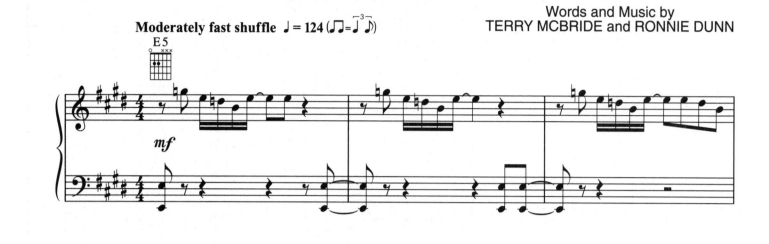

Verse:

1. I got a six - pack, got a
2. See additional lyrics

sin - gle-stem rose.___ My ba - by's dressed up,___ she's rar - ing to go.___ I got a jones___

Beer Thirty - 4 - 1

Verse 2:
I put in my forty, I'm goin' home.
Lord, my get-up, it's got up and gone.
Got my paycheck, I'm on my way.
It's finally Friday, my kind of day.
I punch the clock, I hit the road flyin'.
It's beer thirty, a honky-tonk time.
(To Chorus:)

THE BEST DAY

Words and Music by
CARSON CHAMBERLAIN and DEAN DILLON

The Best Day - 4 - 1

D.S. 𝄋 al Coda

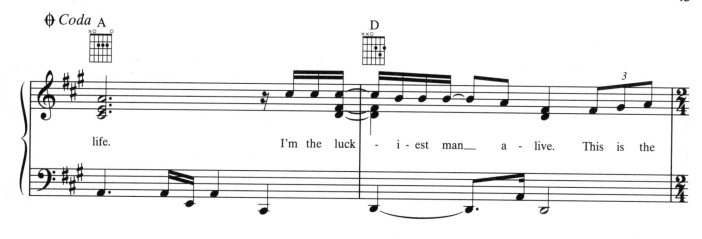

life. I'm the luck - i - est man____ a - live. This is the

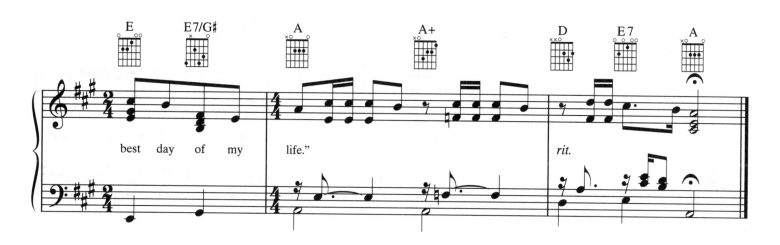

best day of my life." *rit.*

Verse 2:
His fifteenth birthday rolled around,
Classic cars were his thing.
When I pulled in the drive with that old Vette,
I thought the boy would go insane.
When you're in your teens, your dreams revolve
Around four spinnin' wheels.
We worked nights on end, 'til it was new again.
And as he sat behind the wheel, he said,
(To Chorus:)

Chorus 3:
"Dad, this could be the best day of my life.
I've been dreaming day and night of bein' like you.
Now it's me and her.
Watching you and Mom, I've learned
I'm the luckiest man alive
And this is the best day of my life."

BUSY MAN

Words and Music by
GEORGE TEREN
and BOB REGAN

Busy Man - 4 - 1

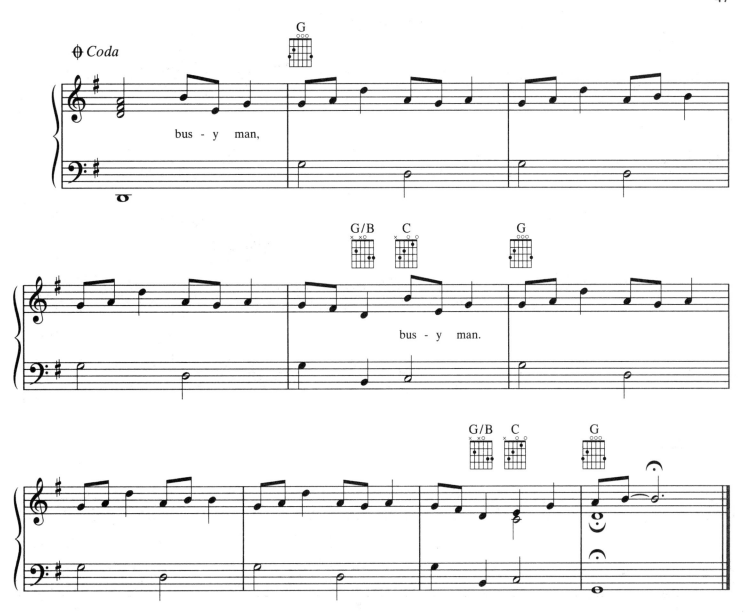

Verse 2:
His sister's out on the sidewalk,
Setting up a lemonade stand.
"Hey, Daddy, don't you want to buy a glass from me?"
You say, "Maybe later; can't you see I'm a busy man?"
(To Chorus 1:)

Verse 3:
There's a woman in the bedroom crying,
Saying, "I thought that we had plans."
You say, "Honey, I'm sorry, I'll make it up
When the job slows down and I'm not such a busy man."
(To Chorus 2:)

Verse 4:
There's a call one day from the office;
They need you down in Birmingham.
You say, "No way, the weekend's mine. I got
Plans with the kids and a date with my wife; I'm a busy man."
(To Chorus 3:)

Chorus 3:
You gotta go, gotta run, take a break and have some fun.
Those that love you most say you've come far.
Got some new priorities in that schedule that you keep.
And when you say that time's a-wasting,
Now you know how right you are, busy man.
(To Coda)

CAN'T NOBODY LOVE YOU
(LIKE I DO)

Words and Music by
DANNY ORTON and CATHY MAJESKI

Can't Nobody Love You (Like I Do) - 4 - 1

Verse 2:
Can't nobody hold you quite this close
All night like I want to.
Baby, put your sweet lips here on mine.
You'll see, 'cause I'm gonna show you
Just how an angel like you should be loved.
Man, I can't feel you enough.
Can't nobody love you like I do.
Can't nobody love you like I do.

THE CHAIN OF LOVE

Music and Lyrics by
JOHNNIE BARNETT and RORY LEE

Moderately slow country two-beat ♩ = 80

(with pedal)

1. He was

℅ *Verses 1 - 4:*

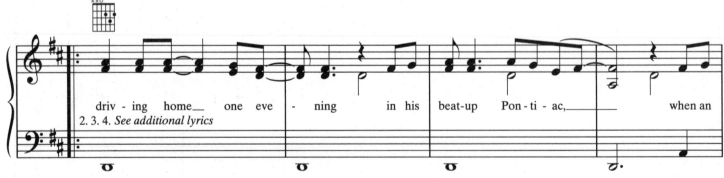

driv-ing home__ one eve-ning in his beat-up Pon-ti-ac,__ when an

2. 3. 4. *See additional lyrics*

old la-dy flagged__ him down. Her Mer-ce-des had__ a flat.__ He could

The Chain of Love - 4 - 1

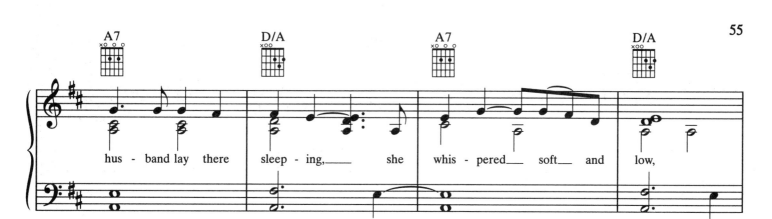

Verse 2:
She said, "I'm from St. Louis,
And I'm only passing through.
I must've seen a hundred cars go by.
This is awful nice of you."
When he'd changed the tire
And closed the trunk,
And was about to drive away,
She said, "How much do I owe you?"
Here's what he had to say:
(To Chorus:)

Verse 3:
Well, a few miles down the road,
The lady saw a small cafe.
She went in to grab a bite to eat
And then be on her way.
But she couldn't help but notice
How the waitress smiled so sweet,
And how she must've been eight months along
And dead on her feet.

Verse 4:
Though she didn't know her story
And she probably never will,
When the waitress went to get her change
From a hundred dollar bill,
The lady slipped right out the door
And on a napkin left a note.
There were tears in the waitress's eyes
When she read what she wrote:
(To Chorus:)

CHANGE

Words and Music by
CRAIG WISEMAN and
MARK SELBY

Change - 4 - 1

Verse 2:
Now, Betty's walking out of a tattoo parlor,
She's got curlers in her hair.
She still can't believe she had a little red rose
Put right on her derriére.
And she's still gotta pick up that red lace teddy
And a bottle of French champagne.
Well, her husband don't know it, but tonight,
Well, he's in for a…
(To Chorus:)

Verse 3:
Now, who of us hasn't been heading home Friday,
Sitting at some traffic light,
Wondering what would happen if we hung a left
Instead of taking that faithful ol' right?
It's the human condition; a part of us wishes
That life wouldn't get so tame.
And we all know better than
Thinking that's ever gonna…
(To Chorus:)

COULDN'T LAST A MOMENT

Words and Music by
DANNY WELLS and JEFFREY STEELE

Moderately ♩ = 96

1. (Spoken:) I thought it was over.
2. See additional lyrics

I thought I could move on, *but I was wrong.*

I woke up last night *calling your name (Sung:) and feel -*

Couldn't Last a Moment - 4 - 1

D.S. ％ al Coda

Verse 2:
(Spoken:)
You've got every right
To turn and walk away.
I can't make you stay.
I broke your heart,
That's the bottom line.
(Sung:)
I wasted so much precious time.
I see you with your friends
Wearing a smile again.
What was I thinking,
Thinking I could still walk down the street…
(To Chorus:)

FAITH IN YOU

Words and Music by
BILL ANDERSON and STEVE WARINER

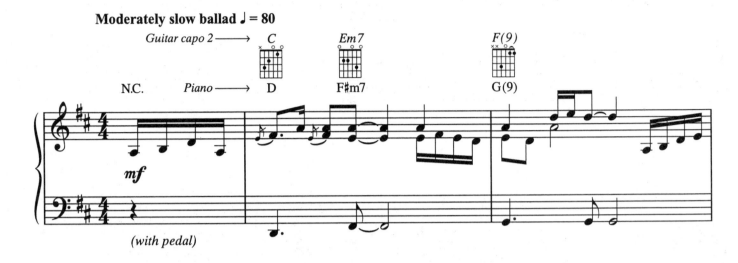

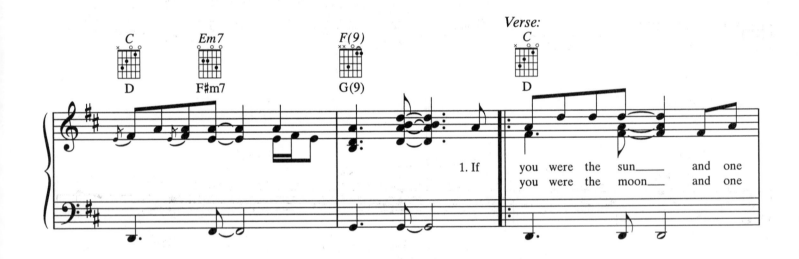

1. If you were the sun___ and one
you were the moon___ and one

day you lost___ all your light___ and you dis-ap-peared, I'd
night a big,___ black___ cloud___ came and cov-ered your face, I'd

Faith In You - 4 - 1

FALLIN' (NEVER FELT SO GOOD)

Words and Music by
SHAWN CAMP and WILL SMITH

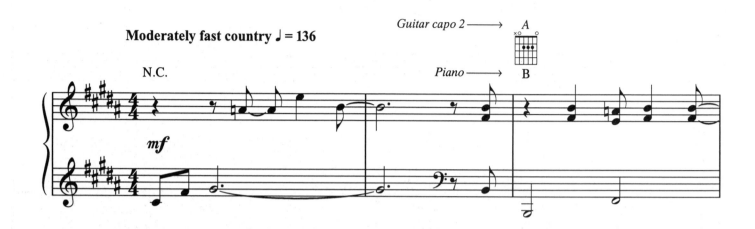

Verse 1:

Fallin' (Never Felt So Good) - 4 - 1

Verse 3:
Who can say what may lie in store,
Smooth sailin' on a sea of love or
Runnin' aground on a rocky shore?
Now that I've found you, I'm not lettin' go,
'Cause I've been searching high and low.
Only one thing that I know:
The higher you take me, the deeper I go.
(To Chorus:)

THE FUN OF YOUR LOVE

Words and Music by
BETH NIELSEN CHAPMAN, JENNIFER DAY
and ANNIE ROBOFF

Moderately ♩ = 96

Verse:

1. Boy, you blow my mind, you can make me
2. *See additional lyrics*

cra-zy. (Make me laugh, make me cry, keep-ing my heart shook up.) I'm so mes-mer-ized,

and you're the one who can save me.
(So sweet and fine, throw me a line.

The Fun of Your Love - 4 - 1

Verse 2:
Now, I've shown you how
I can push the limits.
(I make you laugh, make you cry,
I'm keeping your heart shook up.)
Still you turn me around with sweet forgiveness.
(You draw the line, I'll pay the fine,
That's the sign of a good love.)
In this twisted world we live in,
Please don't stop this love you're giving.
(To Chorus:)

GONE CRAZY

Words and Music by
ALAN JACKSON

Gone Crazy - 4 - 1

Verse 2:
I never saw your face this many times
When you were really here.
The things you said I never understood
Are now crystal clear.
I never spent this much time at home,
But ever since you left, I've been gone.
(To Chorus:)

HANDS OF A WORKING MAN

Words and Music by
DAVID VINCENT WILLIAMS
and JIM COLLINS

Hands of a Working Man - 4 - 1

work-ing man,_____

with the hands   of   a

work-ing man._____

Verse 2:
He stares out the window
And stirs his coffee cup.
Another day, another dollar
Short of catching up.
(To Bridge:)

Verse 3:
Down at the factory,
Standing in line,
He waits to punch the time clock,
A million worries on his mind.
(To Verse 4:)

Verse 4:
Jimmy's needing braces
And Betty's needing time,
And the problems that he's facing,
They're all building up inside.
(To Bridge:)

HOW FOREVER FEELS

Words and Music by
WENDELL MOBLEY and TONY MULLINS

1.†Big, or-ange ball sink-in' in the wa-ter.
2.3. *See additional lyrics*

How Forever Feels - 4 - 1

Verse 2:
Hands on the wheel, cruisiní down the interstate.
Gas pedal breaks and carries my car away.
I was goiní as fast as a Rambler goes.
I could feel the speed from my head to my toes.
Now I know how Richard Petty feels.
(To Chorus:)

Verse 3:
Saved two months, bought a little diamond.
Tonightís the night, feels like perfect timiní.
Down on one knee on her mamaís front steps.
Man, Iím gonna die if she really says yes.
I wanna know how forever feels.
(To Chorus:)

I CAN'T GET OVER YOU

Words and Music by
TERRY McBRIDE
and RONNIE DUNN

I Can't Get Over You - 5 - 5

Verse 2:
I got a front-row seat here to a fool's masquerade,
And that fool in the mirror keeps sayin' I'm doin' OK.
I stare at the door that you walked out.
It hits me hard and leaves no doubt.
(To Chorus:)

I HOPE YOU DANCE

Words and Music by
MARK D. SANDERS and
TIA SILLERS

I Hope You Dance - 5 - 1

Verse 2:
I hope you never fear those mountains in the distance,
Never settle for the path of least resistance.
Livin' might mean takin' chances but they're worth takin'.
Lovin' might be a mistake but it's worth makin'.
(To Chorus 2:)

Chorus 2:
Don't let some hell-bent heart leave you bitter.
When you come close to sellin' out, reconsider.
Give the heavens above more than just a passing glance.
And when you get the choice to sit it out or dance,...
(To Chorus 3:)

I'LL BE

Words and Music by
DIANE WARREN

1. When dark-ness falls_ up-on_ your heart_ and soul,_
2. See additional lyrics

I'll be the light that shines for you._ When you_ for-get_ how beau-

ti-ful_ you are,_ I'll be there to re-mind_ you._ When

I'll Be - 3 - 1

Verse 2:
And when you're there with no one there to hold,
I'll be the arms that reach for you.
And when you feel your faith is running low,
I'll be there to believe in you.
When all you find are lies,
I'll be the truth you need.
When you need someone to run to,
You can run to me.
(To Chorus:)

IT MUST BE LOVE

Words and Music by
BOB McDILL

Verse 2:
Something is wrong, alright,
I think of you all night.
Can't sleep till morning light,
It must be love.
Seeing you in my dreams,
Holding you close to me.
Oh, what else can it be,
It must be love.
(To Chorus:)

I'LL THINK OF A REASON LATER

Words and Music by
TONY MARTIN and TIM NICHOLS

Moderately fast ♩ = 128

Guitar capo 1

1. I heard he was gonna marry some girl from Denver.

2. See additional lyrics

Then my

I'll Think of a Reason Later - 4 - 1

Verse 2:
I drew horns and blacked out a tooth with a marker.
Childish, yes, but she made such a thin, little target.
I couldn't be happier on my own,
But I've got the slightest of a jealous bone,
And seeing her with him tends to enlarge it.
(To Chorus 1:)

Chorus 2:
(Instrumental)
Inside her head may lay all the answers
For curing diseases from baldness to cancer.
Salt of the earth and a real good dancer,
But I really hate her.
I'll think of a reason later.

Spoken:
Well, it was just one tooth.
Did I mention I don't particularly care for her?
She makes me sick.

I'VE FORGOTTEN HOW YOU FEEL

Words and Music by
SONYA ISAACS and KEITH SEWELL

Verse 2:
It's been so long since I heard you say you needed me.
It's hard to hear it, when we never talk at all.
Silence is a heartache; there's just one way to heal.
But, baby, I've forgotten how you feel.
(To Chorus:)

IT WAS

Words and Music by
GARY BURR and MARK WRIGHT

IT'S A BEAUTIFUL THING

Words and Music by
CRAIG WISEMAN and JEFFREY STEELE

It's a Beautiful Thing - 5 - 1

116

Repeat ad lib. and fade

Verse 2:
Daddy's waiting with the bride
As she helps him with his tie.
She sees a tear.
He says, "It's hot in here."
He hugs his little girl and asks,
"How did you grow up so fast?
God, I wish your mama could be here for this."
And everybody stands and smiles
As she comes walking down the aisle
In her mama's gown,
And Daddy breaks on down.
Gran and Gramps in the second row
Stood right there fifty years ago
And said their vows.
I guess it's workin' out.
(To Chorus:)

IT'S ALWAYS SOMETHIN'

Words and Music by
MARV GREEN and AIMEE MAYO

It's Always Somethin' - 5 - 1

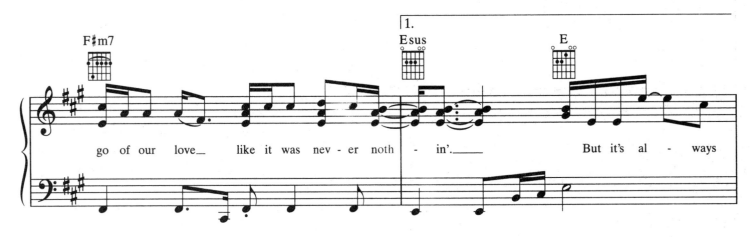

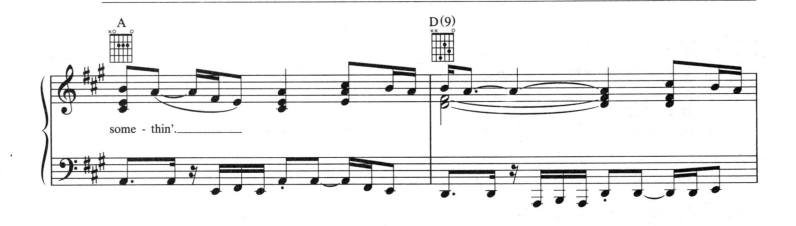

some-thin' ev-'ry day re-mind-in' me,__ ev-'ry-where I go there's a mem-o-ry__ read-

y and a-wait-in' to catch__ me off guard._ There's_ no way__ to pre-pare__ my heart.__ Oh, what_

__ I would-n't give,__ what_ I would-n't do if on - ly I could just stop miss-in' you. I'd let

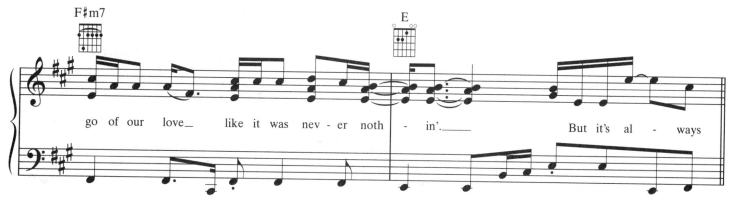

go of our love__ like it was nev-er noth - in'.____ But it's al - ways

some - thin'._____
(Continue vocal ad lib....

Oh,   it's al - ways

Verse 2:
Lunch time, a new place,
Waitress says her name.
Why does it have to be Emily?
Corner store, I stop in.
Someone asks, "How've you been?"
I say, "I wouldn't know.
I really gotta go."
Wish I could forget you
But I don't know how.
'Cause every time I turn around...
(To Chorus:)

KEEPIN' UP

Words and Music by
TEDDY GENTRY, RANDY OWEN,
GREG FOWLER and RONNIE ROGERS

Moderately fast ♩ = 120

mf

Verse:

1. What's go-ing on with the sun___ and the moon?___
2. *See additional lyrics*

Keepin' Up - 5 - 1

Repeat ad lib. and fade

Verse 2:
There's no such thing, for me, as "nine to five."
It takes more sweat than that just to get us by.
It's like I'm chasing my own tail,
'Cause Monday morning starts another stressed-out week.
The world is breathing down my neck; I can feel the heat.
(To Chorus:)

Keepin' Up - 5 - 5

LET'S MAKE SURE WE KISS GOODBYE

Words and Music by
VINCE GILL

Slowly ♩ = 63

1. Kiss me like you'll___ nev-er see my face a-gain,
2.3. *See additional lyrics*

as soft and ten-der___ as you can.

Let's Make Sure We Kiss Goodbye - 3 - 1

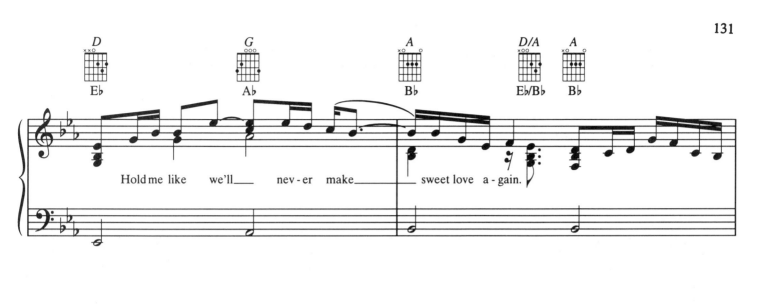

Hold me like we'll___ nev - er make___ sweet love a - gain.

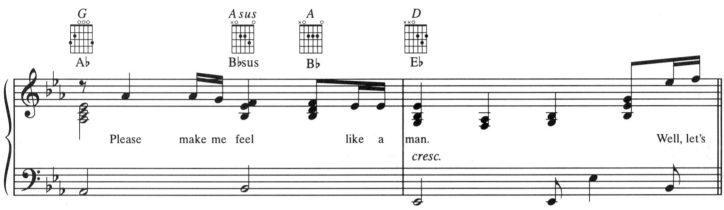

Please make me feel like a man.

cresc.

Well, let's

Chorus:

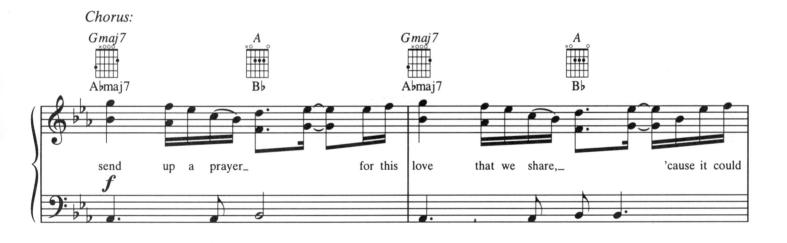

f

send up a prayer_ for this love that we share,_ 'cause it could

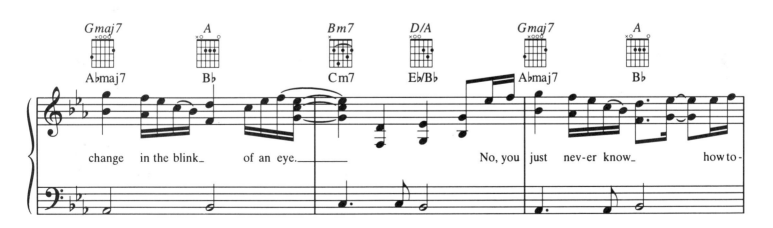

change in the blink_ of an eye.___ No, you just nev-er know_ how to-

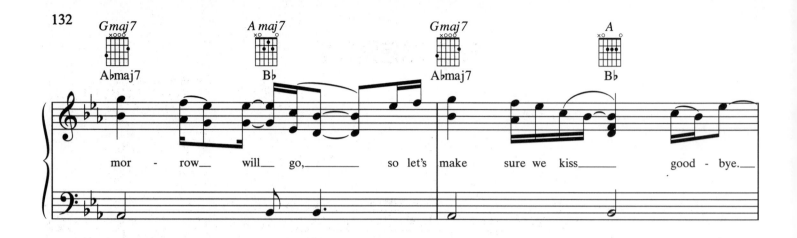

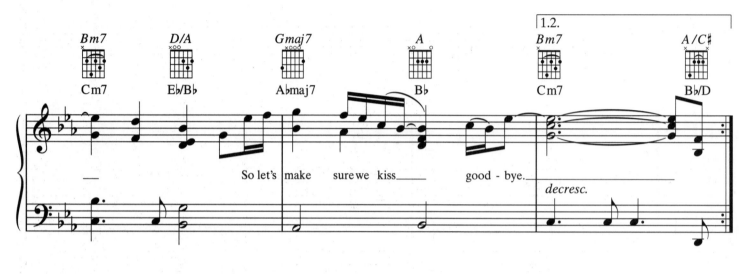

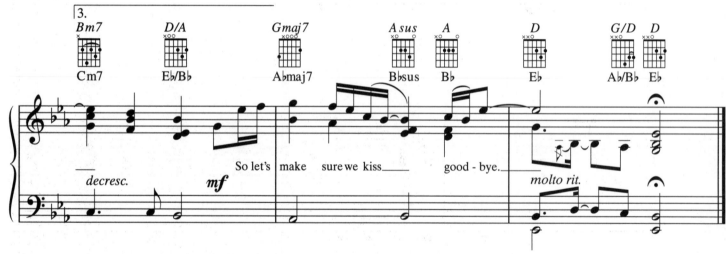

Verse 2:
Look at me just like the day we fell in love
And found the missing pieces to our soul.
You and me have always been just like the birds:
Wherever you are feels like home.
(To Chorus:)

Verse 3:
(Instrumental solo ad lib.)
(To Chorus:)

NO MERCY

Words and Music by
DENNIS MORGAN, STEVE DAVIS
and TODD CERNEY

No Mercy - 5 - 1

Verse 2:
Remember when we thought that bein' apart
Would be the best thing for both our hearts?
It's a prison out there when you're livin' alone, for sure.
Now I know how much I really missed you.
No more games, just wanna be with you.
Just give me all your love till you can't give anymore.
(To Chorus:)

MORE

Words and Music by
THOM MCHUGH and DEL GRAY

1. If an-y-bod-y had told me that an-y-bod-y'd have a hold on me,___

2. *See additional lyrics*

More - 4 - 1

Verse 2:
I can't explain it, I'm more than infatuated.
You got me good, I got it bad.
There's no doubt about it, I can't live without it.
What you got, I just gotta have, so gimme...
(To Chorus:)

(NOW YOU SEE ME) NOW YOU DON'T

Words and Music by
JESS BROWN, TONY LANE
and DAVID LEE

(Now You See Me) Now You Don't - 4 - 1

Verse 2:
If you ever get the feeling that it feels like déjà vu
Because some stranger feels like someone that you know,
Might be the color of her lipstick or the smell of her perfume
That sends a shiver all the way down to your toes.
Don't blink, 'cause it ain't,
Yeah, what you think,
It's just your heart playin' tricks on you.
(To Chorus:)

THE QUITTIN' KIND

Words and Music by
MARK D. SANDERS, SAM HOGIN
and PHIL BARNHART

Verse 1:

1. I know you're hold-in' your breath. You're won-d'rin' what's com-in' next.

The Quittin' Kind - 4 - 1

The Quittin' Kind - 4 - 4

SHE'S MORE

Words and Music by
ROB CROSBY and LIZ HENGBER

She's More - 3 - 1

Verse 2:
No, it wasn't at first sight,
But the moment I looked twice
I saw the woman I was born to love.
Her laughter fills my soul,
And when I hold her, I don't wanna let go.
When it comes to her, I can't get enough.
(To Chorus:)

She's More - 3 - 3

SMOKE RINGS IN THE DARK

Words and Music by
RIVERS RUTHERFORD and HOUSTON ROBERT

Smoke Rings In The Dark - 3 - 1

Verse 2:
The loneliness within me
Takes a heavy toll
'Cause it burns as slow as whiskey
Through an empty, aching soul.
And the night is like a dagger:
Long and cold and sharp.
As I sit here on the front steps,
Blowin' smoke rings in the dark.
(To Chorus:)

Verse 3:
The rain falls where it wants to,
The wind blows where it will.
Everything on earth goes somewhere,
But I swear we're standing still.
So, I'm not gonna wake you.
I'll go easy on your heart.
I'll touch your face and drift away
Like smoke rings in the dark.
(To Chorus:)

Smoke Rings In The Dark - 3 - 3

SOMEBODY'S OUT THERE WATCHING

Words and Music by
ROBIN LERNER, FRANNE GOLDE
and STEVE BOOKER

Moderately ♩ = 72

Somebody's Out There Watching - 7 - 1

Verse:

1. Hope, ev - 'ry - bod - y needs hope,
2. Dreams, ev - 'ry - bod - y needs dreams,

some___ kind of peace of mind___ that they___ can call___ their
all___ the joy and hap - pi - ness___ that the good life

own.___ And ev - 'ry - bod - y needs love,___
brings.___ Ev - 'ry - bod - y needs free - dom.

just___ a lit - tle trust. 'Cause some - times
Ev - 'ry - bod - y needs touch, some - where to

%. Chorus:

some - bod - y's out there watch - ing, some -

bod - y's out there watch - ing. I be - lieve

some -

bod - y's out there watch - ing, some - bod - y's out there watch-

To Coda

ing o - ver me.

Bridge:

Hid - den from us in the sky a - bove us, I can feel it all a - round.

Hard to see it, but I do be - lieve that there are

THIS WOMAN NEEDS

Words and Music by
BONNIE BAKER, KRISTYN OSBORN
and CONNIE HARRINGTON

Verse 2:
This woman needs to be reassured
That my heart's your home
And love is what wills you to stay.
I need you to see me in every light
And hear that you still think
I'm beautiful anyway.
(To Chorus:)

THREE LITTLE TEARDROPS

Words and Music by
FRANK J. MYERS and BUCK MOORE

Three Little Teardrops - 3 - 1

Verse 2:
She doesn't mind cooking dinner for one,
The grocery bill's cheaper these days.
She kinda likes sleeping in her bed alone,
No one pulls the covers away.
Her life's looking better from her point of view,
But sometimes she still has a bad day or two.
(To Chorus:)

WHAT ABOUT NOW

Words and Music by
ANTHONY SMITH, AARON BARKER
and RON HARBIN

What About Now - 5 - 1

Verses 2 & 3:

en hun-dred dol-lars was a heck of a deal__ for a four__ hun-dred horse-pow-er

juke-box on wheels. 2. And that road__ rolls out like a wel - come mat.__ I don't know__

3. *See additional lyrics*

__ where to go,__ but it beats__ where we're at.__ We al - ways said,__ some-day,__

__ some-how,__ we're gon - na get a-way,__ gon - na blow__ this town.__

% *Chorus:*

What a-bout now?__ How 'bout to-night?__ Ba-by, for once,

Verse 3:
We've been putting this off, baby, long enough.
Just give me the word and we'll be kickin' up dust.
We both know it's just a matter of time
Till our hearts start racin' for that county line.
(To Chorus:)

UNBREAKABLE HEART

Words and Music by
BENMONT TENCH

176

Unbreakable Heart - 4 - 3

Verse 2:
In my blue world, you shone like heaven's fire
And left me cryin' in the dark.
How could anyone be so hard?
Did you think I had an unbreakable heart?
(To Bridge:)

Verse 3:
One day, someone will come to you
And rock you tightly in her arms.
Please remember this when you drop your guard:
Nobody has an unbreakable heart.

UNCONDITIONAL

Words and Music by
MELVERN RUTHERFORD, DEANNA BRYANT
and LIZ HENGBER

Slow country ballad ♩ = 72

Unconditional - 4 - 1

WHEN YOU SAY NOTHING AT ALL

Words and Music by
PAUL OVERSTREET and DON SCHLITZ

Lyrics:

It's a-maz-ing how you can speak right to my heart. With-out say-ing a word you can light up my life.

All day long I can hear peo-ple talk-ing out loud. But when you hold me near you drown out the crowd.

When You Say Say Nothing At All - 3 - 1

Try as I may,__ I could nev - er ex-plain__
Old Mis - ter Web - ster could nev - er de-fine__

what I hear__when you don't __ say a thing.__
what's be - ing said __ be - tween your____ heart and mine.__

The

smile on your face__ lets me know__that you need_me. There's a truth in your eyes_say - ing you'll

__ nev- er leave__ me. A touch of your hand_says you'll catch__ me if ev - er I fall.__

To Coda ⊕

Yeah, you say it best__

When You Say Say Nothing At All- 3 - 2